i explore

SPACE

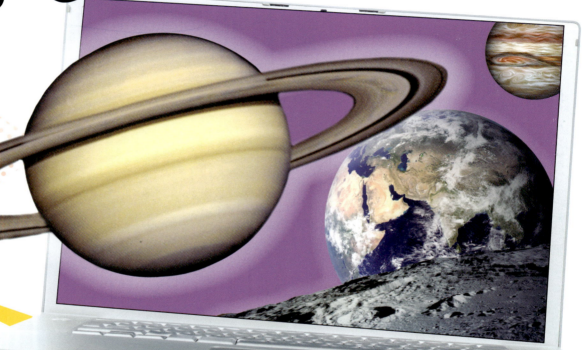

This book belongs to: _____

WHAT'S INSIDE?

Discover more about the amazing world of space!

The Universe	4
The Sun and stars	6
Mercury, Venus & Mars	8
Earth & the Moon	10
Jupiter & Saturn	12
Uranus & Neptune	14
Space exploration	16
International Space Station	18
i explore more & index	20

The Universe

Earth & the Moon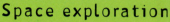

3-D

Throughout this book, you will find 3-D pictures to explore. Look for the 3-D glasses symbol to find them! To view the pictures, remove the 3-D glasses from the book cover and then hold the red lens over your left eye and the blue lens over your right eye. Watch as the picture comes to life!

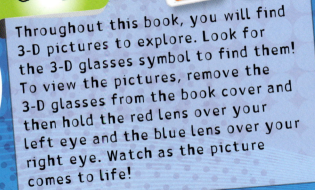

Space exploration

The Sun and stars

Mercury, Venus & Mars

Jupiter & Saturn

Uranus & Neptune

International Space Station

i explore more & index

THE UNIVERSE

The Universe is the name we give to everything that exists, including all of the stars, planets, and galaxies. Scientists believe it began 13.7 thousand, million years ago in a giant explosion called the Big Bang!

i discover

The Universe contains billions of galaxies. A galaxy is a group of stars, dust, and gas, held together by an invisible force called gravity. This force pulls objects together and stops them from flying off into space! There is not enough gravity to hold astronauts down in space – this is why they look like they are floating!

Astronauts in space

The Solar System

i facts

The Solar System is the name we give to our Sun and the planets, moons, comets, and asteroids that circle around it.

We live in a galaxy called The Milky Way, which contains about 200 thousand, million stars.

branching arm

The Milky Way

The Milky Way seen from Earth

i learn

Galaxies come in different shapes. The Milky Way is a spiral-shaped galaxy because the arms that branch out from its center make it look like a spiral.

5

i explore

THE SUN AND STARS

The Sun is the star in the middle of our Solar System. It is a huge ball of extremely hot gas that gives out heat and light. Without the Sun, there would be no life on Earth.

 i discover

The Sun's gravity makes all the planets in our Solar System travel in circular paths around it. These paths are called orbits. The Earth takes one year to complete an orbit around the Sun.

Planets in our Solar System in orbit around the Sun

i learn

A star can live for millions of years. The Sun is actually a medium-sized star, and it will keep giving us heat and light for another five thousand, million years!

Shooting star

i facts

Shooting stars look like flashes of light flying across the sky. They are made up of pieces of ice and rock called meteors.

Some stars look like they make patterns in the sky. We call these patterns constellations.

The Big Dipper, part of The Great Bear

i explore

MERCURY, VENUS, AND MARS

Venus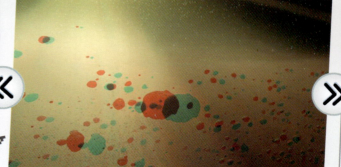

The Inner Solar System is made up of four planets – Mercury, Venus, Earth, and Mars – and the asteroid belt!

i discover

An asteroid is a large piece of rock or metal that is left over from the time when the planets were forming. Most asteroids can be found in orbit between Mars and Jupiter. This area is called the asteroid belt.

Asteroid belt

Mercury

i facts

When Mercury passes between the Earth and the Sun, we see it as a black dot against the Sun's surface. This is called a transit. The next transit is due to happen in 2016.

From Earth, Venus looks like one of the brightest objects in the Solar System. This is because its clouds reflect light from the Sun.

Mars

i learn

Mars is nicknamed the Red Planet. It gets its reddish-brown color from the dust, sand, and rocks on its surface.

red-colored surface

i explore

EARTH AND THE MOON

Earth

Earth is the only planet that we know of on which life exists. It has the perfect combination of temperature, atmosphere, and water. So far, we have only set foot on Earth and the Moon.

The Moon orbiting the Earth

i learn

Objects that orbit a planet or star are called satellites. The Moon is a satellite that circles the Earth. The Moon doesn't give out any light of its own. It shines in the night sky because it reflects the light of the Sun.

i discover

An atmosphere is a layer of gas that surrounds a planet – the Earth's atmosphere makes up the air that we breathe. When a meteor enters Earth's atmosphere, it usually burns up before it hits the ground. The Moon has no atmosphere, so meteors often hit its surface, causing craters.

The Earth's atmosphere

Moon

i facts

Three-quarters of the Earth's surface is covered in water. The deepest point in the ocean is called the Mariana Trench. It is deeper than the height of the world's highest mountain, Mount Everest!

The first men to walk on the moon were Neil Armstrong and Buzz Aldrin in 1969.

crater

Buzz Aldrin on the moon

i explore

JUPITER AND SATURN

The Outer Solar System contains four planets that are made mostly of gas. Jupiter and Saturn are the two largest planets in the Solar System, and scientists call them the gas giants!

Saturn

Jupiter and Ganymede

i facts

- Saturn's moon, Titan, is the only moon in the Solar System to have a thick atmosphere like that of the Earth. However, at -292°F (-180°C), it would be too cold for people to live there!

- Jupiter's moon, Ganymede, is the biggest moon in the Solar System.

i learn

Jupiter is covered in swirling gas clouds, so it looks different every day. The largest gas cloud is called the Great Red Spot. This spot is a storm that is bigger than Earth. Scientists believe that the storm has lasted for hundreds of years.

Great Red Spot

Jupiter

i discover

Saturn's rings are made up of millions of pieces of ice, which are thought to be pieces of an old moon that smashed apart many years ago. Saturn's rings are so long that they could circle the Earth more than 44 times!

Pieces of ice from Saturn's rings

URANUS AND NEPTUNE

Uranus and Neptune are the two planets farthest away from the Sun. Uranus is a blue-green color, while Neptune is bright blue. These colors come from a gas called methane in the planets' atmospheres.

poles

Uranus

Uranus is at a different angle to all the other planets – its poles look as though they are on its sides. Scientists think that long ago, Uranus may have collided with another planet causing it to lean this way.

Uranus and five of its 27 moons

i facts

Like Jupiter and Saturn, Uranus and Neptune are nicknamed the gas giants. They are also called the ice giants because they contain lots of ice!

Uranus has 27 moons! The biggest moons are called Oberon and Titania.

Neptune

Great Dark Spot

i discover

Neptune's environment is very harsh, with winds that are 9 times stronger than the winds on Earth. A spacecraft called Voyager 2 found a storm on Neptune that was traveling at 750 mph (1,200 kph). Scientists called this the Great Dark Spot.

Voyager 2

i explore

SPACE EXPLORATION

The first man in space was a Russian named Yuri Gagarin, who orbited Earth in 1961. Since then, humans have been exploring space in new and amazing ways!

i facts

Galileo was one of the first astronomers. His telescope was powerful enough to see the craters on the Moon, but very weak compared to today's electronic telescopes.

The Spirit and Opportunity rovers were machines that landed on Mars in 2004. They sent vital information back to Earth, proving that Mars once had water.

Rover on Mars

helmet

visor

spacesuit

i discover

One of the most powerful telescopes today is the Hubble telescope, which orbits the Earth. It can see far beyond our Solar System and has taken photos of the most distant galaxies in the Universe!

The Hubble telescope

i learn

When astronauts are in space, they wear a spacesuit that protects them from the cold and provides air for them to breathe. A thin layer of gold on the helmet's visor ensures that the Sun's rays do not harm the astronaut's eyes.

i explore

INTERNATIONAL SPACE STATION

Since November 2000, astronauts have been living in the International Space Station. This is a spacecraft that orbits the Earth. Up to six people can live there at a time.

 **i learn**

On the space station, astronauts carry out experiments, make repairs and observe the Earth and space. Astronauts also complete spacewalks, which is when they leave the space station, to carry out experiments or repairs in space!

astronaut   robonaut

Robonaut 2

solar panels

The Cupola

i discover

The space station doesn't just have people on board – it also has a robot! Robonaut 2 is a test robot that looks and moves just like a human. Scientists hope it is the first step towards creating robots that can help people in space and on Earth.

i facts

The space station is powered by four sets of solar panels, which together are the size of 15 tennis courts!

The space station has an observation deck called the Cupola. This is where astronauts watch the work happening outside the spacecraft.

19

i explore more

ℹ The first living thing to travel into space was a dog! Laika the dog traveled in a spacecraft called Sputnik II on a mission to find out whether living things could survive space travel.

If somebody shouted at you in space, you wouldn't be able to hear them – even if they shouted in your ear! This is because there's no air to carry the sound.

The largest galaxy we know of contains more than 100 million, million stars!

If you could find a swimming pool big enough to fit Saturn in, it would float on water!

Mercury rotates on its axis much more slowly than Earth, which means that one day on Mercury would last 59 days on Earth!

You should never look right at the Sun – it would damage your eyes.

index

asteroid 5, 8
asteroid belt 8
astronaut 4, 16, 17, 18, 19
atmosphere 10, 11, 12, 14

crater 11, 16

Earth 6, 8, 9, 10-11, 12, 13, 15, 16, 17, 18, 19, 20
exploration 16-17

galaxy 4, 5, 17, 20
gravity 4, 6

International Space Station 18-19

Jupiter 12-13

Mars 8-9, 16
Mercury 8-9, 20
moon 5, 10-11, 12, 13, 15, 16

Neptune 14-15
orbit 6, 10, 17

Saturn 12-13, 20
Solar System 5, 6, 8, 12, 17
spacecraft 15, 18, 20
spacesuit 17
star 4, 5, 6, 7, 20
Sun 5, 6-7, 9, 14, 17, 20

telescope 16, 17

The Milky Way 5

Universe 4-5
Uranus 14-15

Venus 8-9